ED NORTON'S
SECRETS TO
THE MEANING
OF LIFE

ED NORTON'S SECRETS TO THE MEANING OF LIFE

Peter Crescenti

Rutledge Hill Press

Nashville, Tennessee

Published in Nashville, Tennessee, by Rutledge Hill Press, Inc.,
513 Third Avenue South, Nashville, Tennessee 37210.

Typography by D&T/Bailey Typesetting, Inc.,
Nashville, Tennessee
Design by Harriet Bateman

Library of Congress Cataloging-in-Publication Data

Crescenti, Peter.
    Ed Norton's secrets to the meaning of life/Peter Crescenti.
        p. cm.
    ISBN 1-55853-177-7
    1. Honeymooners (Television program) 2. Norton, Ed
(Fictitious character) 3. American wit and humor. I. Title.
PN1992.77.H623C63   1992
791.45'72 — dc20   92-15787
                                                         CIP

Printed in the United States of America
1 2 3 4 5 6 7 — 97 96 95 94 93 92

To

Marvin Marx & Walter Stone
Leonard Stern & Syd Zelinka
Herb Finn & A. J. Russell

The men who put the skin on the bones
and the words in the mouths
of the funniest characters
in television history.

**A sincere "Thank You" to all those
who helped make this book possible:**

Larry Stone and Ron Pitkin, Rutledge Hill Press
Howard Berk, Viacom
Denise Marcil, Denise Marcil Literary Agency
MPI Home Video and CBS Video Library
Mike Nejad, photographer
"Daddy" and Howard Frank, Personality Photos Inc.

"Blessed is the man who trusts in the Lord,
whose confidence is in him."
Jeremiah 17:7

CONTENTS

INTRODUCTION

Space cadet, full-grown nut, mental case…these are just a few of the phrases that have been used to describe Ed Norton, Ralph Kramden's best pal, America's favorite upstairs neighbor and the only guy that could make the sewer seem like a great place to work.

Playing in "The Honeymooners" opposite Ralph — his antithesis in every way except gullibility — Norton is the epitome of the lovable dope, the good-natured slob, the sucker born every minute. With his predilection for comic books, junk food, and kiddie television, he is the Simple Simon of subterranean sanitation, Peter Pan with a screw loose. Brooklyn is his Never-Never Land; he won't grow up, and that's that.

The refreshing things about Norton are his innocence and good humor. He knows he's a kid in a man's body and it doesn't bother him one bit. He's happy as he is and aspires to nothing more. He wears a Mickey Mouse watch with pride. He has his Howdy Doody T-shirt laundered because he doesn't trust his wife with it. He is as upset about missing an episode of "Captain Video and His Video Rangers" as he is about losing his job.

Unlike Ralph, Norton manages the responsibilities of daily life without letting them drain his zest for living. He works an eight-hour day like everybody else, but when the whistle blows he's like a kid without a care in the world. Knocking off pizzas like they were hors d'oeuvres, watching Charlie Chan movies on the "Late, Late, Late Show," shooting pool, hanging out at the Racoon Lodge. This is the good life à la Norton, without pretentions and the high price tag.

Norton's makeup makes him the perfect foil for Ralph. Much of their relationship consists of Ralph conning Norton, insulting him or sizing him up for a straitjacket. A psychologist might suggest that Norton is a masochist for taking it, but Norton would simply tell you that sticks and stones may break his bones, but names will never hurt him.

The real Norton lies somewhere between a fascinating case study and a common numskull. Though we may question the sanity of a guy who thinks he can get out of taking his wife to Atlantic City by telling her it's closed for the summer, we also have to admire Norton for his ability to keep the sheer mass of Ralph's ego at bay with his quick wit. Whether it's a defense mechanism, a mean streak, or just childish clowning, Norton even outclasses Alice when it comes to letting the hot air out of Ralph's balloon.

Neither does Norton have an equal when it comes to patently stupid remarks. When Ralph wants to get rid of Alice's visiting aunt, Norton tells him to yell "Fire." When Ralph reminds him that the other people in the building will think there's a fire too, Norton simply revises his suggestion and tells Ralph to yell "Fire, Aunt Ethel." As Ralph so appropriately put it, "This is the man they can't do without down in the sewer!"

Speaking of the sewers, Norton has singlehandedly put them "on the map," so to speak. Much of Norton's humor derives from his work, and one begins to wonder if maybe his brain hasn't become waterlogged from spending too much time underground. How else do you explain a man who wants to put his son through college... and then use his connections to get him a job in the sewer? Well, if nothing else, Norton would be carrying on a proud family tradition — there have been Nortons underground ever since there were sewers!

With his wit sharpened by rubbing it against Ralph's

abrasive personality, Norton always has a ready wise-crack for his wife, Trixie, his second favorite target. Though he seems to be happily married, Norton has more than a few knocks for the institution. On the other hand, if Trixie's cooking is as bad as Norton says it is — why would a guy who loves to eat as much as he does joke about a thing like that? — it's no wonder that Norton spends so much time eating at the Kramdens'.

Whatever the reason and whomever the target, Norton is never at a loss for words. And it is his words — which take the form of wacko ideas, fat jokes, "underground" wisdom, and psycho-philosophy — that have made him the most beloved full-grown nut in the world.

ED NORTON'S
SECRETS TO
THE MEANING
OF LIFE

PAL O' MINE

Ralph: Just remember Norton, when there's an emergency, I come out of it. When they made me they threw away the mold.
Norton: They had to...you probably broke it.

Norton defends his honor.

Ralph: That's the difference between you and me. *I* am a boss. *You* are a mouse.
Norton: I'd rather be a live mouse than a dead boss!

Ralph has an appointment with the IRS.

Ralph: Don't you realize how serious this is? They're investigating me!
Alice: Ralph, being investigated is not the end of the world. You are not the first person who was ever investigated.
Norton: You're darn right. The jails are full of 'em.

Ralph reminisces.

Norton: As long as I can remember I weighed exactly what I weigh now, a hundred and sixty-five pounds.
Ralph: Gee, I remember when I used to weigh a hundred and sixty-five. Did you ever see a picture of me when I weighed a hundred and sixty-five pounds?
Norton: No Ralph, I never did see any of your baby pictures.

Ralph has hurt his back bowling.

Norton: The way you were standing there you looked like the Leaning Tower of Pizza.
Ralph: Pisa! Pisa!
Norton: It may be Pisa but I know pizza when I see it.

Alice wants to get rid of Ralph's old cornet.

Alice: You haven't touched it in years.
Ralph: I wanna keep it.
Norton: He's right, Alice. He hasn't touched his toes in years either, he still wants to keep them.

I take back my offer to you of a job in the sewer.
Besides, you wouldn't even fit in the manhole!

A reporter is interviewing Norton for an article about Ralph.

Reporter: Tell me, how long ago did you meet?
Norton: Oh, I'd say a hundred and fifty pounds ago.

Ralph's in a bind.

Norton: Let's review the case. Alice wants you to go to the wedding, right?
Ralph: Right.
Norton: You wanna go to the World Series game with me.
Ralph: Right.
Norton: The game and the wedding take place at the same time, right?
Ralph: Right.
Norton: So if you go to one, you miss out on the other, right?
Ralph: Right.
Norton: And Alice says you gotta go to the wedding, right?
Ralph: Right. Well?
Norton: Wait a minute, I'm thinkin'. Now who am I gonna get to go to the game with me Sunday?

Ralph wants to go into hiding rather than fight a bully.

Ralph: Don't treat me like a baby, Alice. If I wanna go outta town, I'll go outta town. You don't have to worry about me, I can take care of myself.
Norton: If you knew how to take care of yourself you wouldn't have to leave town.

The Kramdens have been arguing about whether Ralph will go to the World Series or Alice's sister's wedding.

Norton: You kept me awake all last night.
Ralph: Did you hear it?
Norton: Did I hear it? The top floor is laying eight to five that you go to the wedding.

Ralph has tickets to a Broadway show.

Ralph: Now c'mon Norton, do you wanna go or don't ya? I can't use two seats.
Norton: That's a matter of opinion.

Ralph thinks he's dying of a rare disease and wants to sell his story to a magazine.

Ralph: I can see it now, the first installment... "Doomed Man Has Only Six Months to Go."
Norton: I think that's a little lengthy for the title. They'll probably make it shorter, like "In Six Months, Blimp Takes Off!"

Norton's stickball team needs a new infielder.

Stickball player: How about it, Mr. Kramden. Do you think you could cover second base?

Norton: My boy, you are looking at a man that could cover the infield, the outfield, and four sections of the bleachers.

Ralph's boss wants him to see a psychiatrist.

Ralph: All last night I couldn't sleep a wink. All I kept seein' was guys in white coats running after me tryin' to put me in a straitjacket.

Norton: Don't worry, Ralphie boy. Nobody's gonna put you in a straitjacket.

Ralph: Thank you, Norton.

Norton: Where they gonna find one big enough?

Pour away mein host!

Ralph wants to borrow money.

Norton: It's not that I'm against lending you money. And you could do anything you want with it. It's just what you *don't* do with it.
Ralph: What don't I do with it?
Norton: You don't pay me back.

Ralph is playing matchmaker for an old school chum.

Ralph: What kind of a guy are you? You're quiet, you're easy goin', you're generous, you're considerate, you're the kind of a guy that would appreciate the things a wife would do for ya. Now who do I know who'd want a husband like that?
Norton: How about Alice?

Ralph wants to rent a new apartment.

Woman: Now, you and your wife don't have wild parties, with drinking or dancing?
Ralph: Oh, no.
Norton: He hasn't even taken his wife out in the last five years.

Ralph is trying to write a lullaby but Norton won't accompany him on the piano.

Ralph: If you can play music you can play any kind of music.

Norton: Oh yeah? Name me one rumba that Beethoven wrote.

Ralph, Norton, and some friends are playing poker.

Ralph: Why don't we knock off, it's gettin' kinda late.
Friend: Whaddya mean knock off, I'm out fifteen
bucks. You're the only winner Ralph, give me a chance
for a comeback.
Ralph: What d'you want from me? When we started
playin' we said we're gonna knock off at twelve and its
two o'clock already.
Friend: Well, why didn't we quit at twelve?
Norton: Ralph was losin' then.

YOU SPACE CADET!

The four of us get along like the Three Musketeers.

YOU SPACE CADET!

Ralph has bought Alice a Christmas present.

Ralph: At one time this was in the house of the Emperor of Japan. It was smuggled into this country. I just can't wait to see the expression on her face when she gets this.

Norton: I'd like to see the expression on the Emperor of Japan's face when he finds out it's missing.

Ralph thinks he's dying of a strange disease.

Ralph: Look, Norton, you gotta promise me one thing. I don't want you to tell Alice anything about this.

Norton: All right, all right. But what's gonna happen after six months…she's gonna notice you're not comin' home nights.

Ralph thinks Alice is leaving him for another man.

Ralph: What is the matter with you? Here my home is being broken up, my happiness destroyed, and you wanna know if I'm ready to go bowling.

Norton: Oh, I'm sorry Ralph. How about shootin' a little pool?

Ralph describes to Alice how Norton answered a question on a civil service test.

Ralph: It was one of those questions where you have a choice of what you want to answer. It said if you were heating your own home and oil was twelve cents a gallon and it went up seven percent, and coal at the same time was fourteen dollars a ton and that went up nine percent, what would you do? Whaddya think Norton says? Pack up and move to Florida!

Ralph and Norton are going to make dinner.

Norton: Men are the best chefs, aren't they? Oscar at the Waldorf, Pierre at the Ritz, Grace Kelly's father.
Ralph: What does Grace Kelly's father got to do with it?
Norton: He cooked up a pretty sweet dish!

Norton has been bird watching.

Ralph: Why are you sure it's a yellow-bellied sapsucker?
Norton: What else could it be, it's got a yellow belly and it was suckin' sap!

Norton and Trixie disagree over a gift for one of Norton's buddies.

Norton: I happen to know that Jim McKeever has a weakness for red suspenders.
Alice: Ed, I think Trixie's right. A man would rather have a ring than suspenders.
Norton: Not if his pants are always falling down.

Norton stays for dinner.

Ralph: I thought you already ate.
Norton: Let's face it, Ralph. Dizzy Dean warms up in the bullpen before the game, but he still pitches.

Ralph and Norton are rehearsing a mind-reading act.

Norton: If I'm blindfolded, how'm I gonna know what the object is?
Ralph: It's very simple, I give you a clue. For instance, if I take a watch from 'em I say "*Watch* out for this, oh swami!"
Norton: What's the clue?

Norton advises Ralph on how to make up with Alice.

Norton: You walk in with flowers, candy, smooth shave — you know, the skin a woman loves to touch — it'll work.
Ralph: But suppose it doesn't work?
Norton: Whaddya got to lose? You can smell the flowers, eat the candy, and tomorrow morning you don't have to shave.

Norton has had "words" with his boss.

Norton: After what he told me I find it impossible for me to work one more day for him in the sewer.
Alice: What'd he tell ya?
Norton: You're fired!

Ralph has found a suitcase stuffed with money on his bus.

Ralph: Who coulda left it there? It must've been some millionaire or somethin'.
Norton: Boy, I hope so. I hate to think it was some poor person who could really need it.

Norton has invited the Kramdens to an antique show.

Alice: Since when did you become interested in antiques?

Norton: I'll tell you how it happened. I was in the market for a dog, so I was looking in the paper and I seen this ad, "For Sale, genuine four-legged Chippendale." So I sent away for it, and it came back a table!

Norton's making plans.

Norton: We are gonna make a trip that I've always wanted to make.

Alice: A trip?

Norton: Goin' on a second honeymoon to Niagara Falls…only this time we ain't hitchhikin'.

Ralph thinks he's lost his job.

Ralph: Today I'm fired, tomorrow I'm forgotten. They probably won't even remember what I look like!

Norton: That's all right. You go there tomorrow morning and apply for another job.

Ralph is eating a salad, Norton a pizza.

Ralph: Everything on here is good for ya. Got carrots for your eyes, beets for your blood, there's lettuce for your teeth. Everything's good for something on this plate.
Norton: Poor little pizza, ain't good for nothing.

Ralph is waiting to meet an IRS agent he thinks is investigating him.

Ralph: What am I worried about? I'm an American citizen, got my rights. I'm a taxpayer.
Norton: If you were a taxpayer you wouldn't be down here right now.

Ralph's membership drive at the Racoon Lodge has been a flop.

Norton: I think that we owe him a vote of thanks for the vast improvement made over last year's membership drive.

Racoon president: But he didn't bring in one new member.

Norton: I know. But last year we lost three of the old members.

A stranger has given Norton a handout.

Ralph: Doesn't that surprise you, that a total stranger should come walkin' by, stop, take a look at you, put a quarter in your hand and say "Good luck."

Norton: To tell you the truth I do wonder about it once in a while, Ralph. It happens maybe two, three times a month.

Ralph: You won't have to wonder about it again because I'm gonna tell you why it happens two or three times a month. You look like a bum!

Norton: How d'ya like that, a total stranger! Trixie's whole family thinks I'm a bum and they never give me nothin'!

Ralph is trying to impress an old friend by using his boss's office to pose as the head of the bus company.

Norton: When I bring him up here remember, you are the president of the Gotham Bus Company, not a driver. So don't give yourself away by yelling "Step to the rear of the office."

The Racoon Lodge is going broke.

Ralph: Did you hear what happened yesterday? The Acme Finance Company come in and took out the pool table. The day before that they took out the television set and the phonograph. The day before that they took out the piano. What're we gonna do, Norton?
Norton: Well, we could hold our meetings at the Acme Finance Company.

A mailman spots Ralph and Norton tampering with a mailbox.

Mailman: That's a federal offense. You can get three years in jail for that or a thousand dollar fine.
Norton: How about that, Ralph, you got a choice.

Norton is teaching Ralph how to box.

Ralph: Whaddya tell me to cover up my face and hit me in the stomach for?!?

Norton: Well, that'll teach ya never to trust *anybody* in the ring.

Ralph finds the guest list for a surprise party.

Ralph: She didn't forget my birthday. She's even gonna run me a party!

Norton: Yeah. It's too bad you're not gonna be here to enjoy it.

Ralph: Whaddya mean I'm not gonna be here?

Norton: You're not invited. Your name ain't on the list.

Norton advises Ralph, who thinks he's being investigated by the IRS.

Norton: When you get down there tomorrow stand on the Eighteenth Amendment.
Ralph: Stand on the Eighteenth Amendment? You mean stand on the Fifth Amendment. The Eighteenth Amendment was for prohibition.
Norton: That's just what I mean. Tell 'em you were *drunk* when you made out your taxes!

Norton recalls his glory days.

Norton: I don't think you know this, but I was in the fight game myself. I entered the Golden Gloves, took it pretty serious too. Up every mornin' six o'clock, fifteen-mile jaunt through the park, then box with my sparrin' partner till after lunch, then after lunch skip rope, then chop wood, hit the heavy punchin' bag, hit the light bag, and then to top it all off a twenty-mile hike. I did that every day for three months.
Ralph: Sounds pretty tough. How'd you make out?
Norton: Not so good. I was the only fighter ever carried *into* the ring.

Ralph's discouraged about not getting ahead.

Ralph: If you don't have any connections you get nowhere.
Norton: I don't think that applies to every case. I didn't have no connections when I got my job in the sewer.

Ralph thinks Alice is having an affair, and he has a plan to catch her red-handed.

Norton: You're not gonna stoop so low to go out on the fire escape and spy on your wife, are ya? That went out with the Stone Age, when people were uncivilized. You just can't do a thing like that today.
Ralph: Well, what am I gonna do?
Norton: Do what any civilized man would do...hide a Dictaphone here in the room.

Ralph thinks he has an incurable disease.

Ralph: Well, that's it, Norton. In six months I'll be dead.

Norton: Doctors can be wrong too, you know. How about a friend of mine, a doctor examined him, gave him only six months to live too. Boy he made a monkey outta that doctor.

Ralph: What happened?

Norton: He lived for almost eight months!

The Racoon Lodge has financial problems.

Racoon: What's the reason for the deficit?

Ralph: No one's payin' their dues, that's the reason.

Racoon president: This can't go on, something must be done.

Norton: Mr. President, I have a well-thought-out plan for cutting the deficit that I'd like to offer. As we all know the club dues are two dollars a month and even at that the club members have not been paying their dues. I see no reason why we can't cut the dues down to a dollar a month. Even then, if the members don't pay their dues it will be cutting the deficit in half!

Hello ball!

Ralph and Norton are trying to raise money for a scheme.

Norton: I loaned a guy some money last week. I'll call him up.
Ralph: Hey, that's great.
Norton: Wait a minute, maybe it's not such a good idea after all.
Ralph: Whaddya mean?
Norton: It'll cost me a dime to call 'im...he only owes me a nickel.

Norton is posing as a doctor to help Ralph out of a fix with a magazine.

Magazine editor: Just exactly where do you practice medicine?

Norton: Oh, I don't have to practice it, I know it.

Ralph is making out a will because he thinks he has six months to live.

Ralph: By the way, Norton, I won't forget you in my will. I'm leavin' you my bowling shoes.
Norton: Boy, thanks pal. You know, I was just gonna go out and buy myself a new pair of bowling shoes. This couldn'ta happened at a better time!

Ralph wants to wiggle out of a night out with Alice.

Ralph: All I have to do is start an argument with her, make her so mad that she won't want to go out with me New Year's Eve.
Norton: That's a good idea. Make it a big fight and take care of her birthday too.

Ralph has bought a house and he wants Norton to sign a ninety-nine year lease as his tenant.

Ralph: Sign that thing!
Norton: If you don't mind, Ralph, I'd just like to take my time. I mean, ninety-nine years is a *pretty bit chunk* out of a man's life.

Alice invites Norton for breakfast.

Alice: You want some coffee?

Norton: No, I already had breakfast.

Alice: How about a second breakfast?

Norton: I already had that too. It would be kinda ridiculous to have three breakfasts, wouldn't it?

Alice: Yeah.

Norton: I tell you what I will do, though, I'll start on my first lunch.

Alice's aunt is visiting.

Ralph: I'm goin' crazy, Norton, I gotta get her outta this house.

Norton: I got an idea. Why don't you stick your head out the window and holler "Fire!"

Ralph: How about the rest of the people in the building, they'll think it's on fire for real.

Norton: It's very simple...just yell "Fire, Aunt Ethel!"

Ralph has bought a house and Norton's his tenant. They're discussing a clause in the lease.

Ralph: Even when the ninety-nine years is up I can't throw you out because you got an option in here to renew.

Norton: Well, I'm certainly glad to hear that because when I get to be a hundred and forty-two years old, I won't have to go out and look for a new place to live.

Ralph's griping about paying his taxes.

Norton: Ralph, you got the wrong attitude. The government tries to be very helpful. Take this here joint income tax. That's very convenient.
Ralph: What's convenient about joint income tax?
Norton: Well, that way the husband and wife can go to prison together.

Ralph and Norton are applying for a loan.

Banker: Your mother's name, Mr. Norton.
Norton: Mrs. Norton.
Ralph: He means your mother's name before she was married.
Norton: How do I know? Ever since I know her she's been married.

Ralph and Norton have front-row seats to a prize fight.

Ralph: We'll be sittin' amongst all the fight celebrities. Marciano, Jake LaMotta, Rocky Graziano, LaStarza, Giardello.
Norton: Boy, what a spot for a pizzeria.

Trixie's complaining to Alice about Norton.

Trixie: He didn't even graduate from public school.
Norton: Listen, listen. It wasn't that I was stupid. What could I do, it was the teacher's word against mine.

Their wives won't give Ralph and Norton money for a new scheme.

Ralph: I don't understand it. Trixie won't let you have the money. Alice won't let me have the money. Women certainly are stupid.
Norton: Yeah, especially the ones that married us.

Norton can't keep his mouth shut.

Norton: You're gonna be plenty surprised when Ralph comes home and tells ya that him and me is plannin' to buy a summer cottage for the four of us, and it's only gonna cost nine hundred and eighty-nine dollars.
Alice: You and him are buying what for who and it's only gonna cost how much?
Norton: I can't tell ya, it's a secret!

Tickets for the Racoon Lodge dance are not selling.

Ralph: You mean to tell me you guys haven't sold one ticket?!?
Norton: I'd like to report that I have the promise of one "possible maybe."
Ralph: Well, up to now we got ten people comin' to the dance, and that's the band.
Norton: I'd like to say that I hope the band is there because if my "possible maybe" shows up he wants to dance.

Ralph thinks Alice is seeing another man.

Ralph: Fourteen years I fractured myself drivin' that bus just to take care of her. And what happens? I see her get into a cab with another guy and drive off. That's loyalty for ya.

Norton: Hmm. I mean the least she coulda done is take a bus.

Ralph has won first prize in a contest.

Ralph: We're goin' to Europe!

Norton: Boy Ralph, you and me are gonna have a swell time in Paris!

Ralph: I'm not takin' you, I'm takin' Alice.

Norton: Well, you won't have as much fun in Paris.

Ralph thinks he's been hired for an important job.

Ralph: A guy gets on my bus, he discovers me. Same thing can happen to you, Norton, you just gotta keep pluggin' away. Some day some guy'll discover you.

Norton: Not unless he accidently falls down an open manhole.

Ralph has arranged a date between the neighborhood butcher and Alice's aunt.

Ralph: Have I forgotten anything? Is there anything else I can do to make him feel at home?
Norton: Well, you could sprinkle a little sawdust on the floor and hang a tongue in the window.

Norton has a plan to get a woman out of a telephone booth Ralph wants to use.

Norton: Next door there's a barber shop, there's a phone booth in there. We go in there, get on that phone there and call up this lady here in this phone booth, tell her she's wanted home immediately, it's urgent. She leaves, we come back in here and we use the phone...!

Ralph and Norton need an idea for a song.

Norton: Let's attack it from a different angle, maybe like a combination of somethin' we do every day.
Ralph: Hey, that's right, somethin' that we're familiar with, an expression.
Norton: Wait a minute, I got it. It's a combination of your job and my job, somethin' we do and say every day and the title'll make a great hit.
Ralph: What is it?
Norton: "Please Step to the Rear of the Sewer!"

Ralph and Norton think one of their wives is pregnant.

Ralph: A wife takes her own sweet time tellin' her husband about a thing like that. You can't walk up to a woman that's havin' a baby and say, "Are you havin' a baby?"

Norton: Then we'll find out which one *isn't* havin' a baby and ask *her.*

Ralph needs money because he thinks he's going to be a father.

Norton: At a time like this anything I have is yours.

Ralph: Gee, that's awful nice of you, pal. How much y'got?

Norton: Well, I don't have any cash but I got eighteen bucks owed to me and if I can lay my hands on it, it's yours.

Ralph: You're a pal, Norton. Who owes you?

Norton: You do.

Ralph has entered a contest.

Norton: Take it from one who knows, you're wastin' your time. All those contests are crooked.
Ralph: Whaddya mean, crooked?
Norton: I was in a contest once, you had to name all the states. I got gypped right out of the first prize. I named sixty-six states and the guy that won only named forty-eight!

Norton's in a rut.

Ralph: Tell me somethin', when you go to work, whaddya take with you for lunch?
Norton: Please don't bring it up. The same old thing every day, peanut butter sandwiches, peanut butter sandwiches, and more peanut butter sandwiches. I'm tellin' ya, it's terrible, Ralph!
Ralph: Then why don't you complain to Trixie about it?
Norton: What for, I make my own sandwiches!

The annual Racoon Lodge dance appears to be a flop — again.

Racoon president: In 1953 we lost seventy-eight dollars, in 1954 we lost ninety-two dollars, in 1955 we lost two hundred and eight dollars. Something has got to be done.

Racoon: I suggest we stop running dances.

Norton: What're you crazy, stop running dances? That's the only why we got of makin' any money!

After Ralph helps capture a killer that got on his bus, a crooked politician wants him to run for local office.

Ralph: This could only be the beginning. He said, "Who knows, someday you might be senator, then governor, and one of these days you might even become president." Imagine, me becoming president just because I saw Bullets Durgom on my bus.
Norton: Whaddya know, Ralph. If instead of gettin' on your bus Bullets fell through an open manhole, maybe I could've gotten to be president.

Ralph has won big in a card game and he doesn't want Alice to know.

Ralph: Where could I hide this dough so she won't find it?
Norton: I got an idea. Hide it under the rug.
Ralph: We don't have a rug.
Norton: Well, take the money you won from playin' poker, go out and buy a rug, and then you'll have a place to hide it.

Norton's sick of losing.

Norton: Every single time I play cards I lose. Then I go upstairs and tell Trixie I lost, she gets mad at me, she hollers at me, I go to bed I'm all nervous, I can't sleep. Then the next day at work I'm sick all day!
Ralph: If you get sick, whaddya play all the time for?
Norton: It's the only fun I get!

NOTES FROM THE UNDER-GROUND

The sewers have always been good to me.

NOTES FROM THE UNDERGROUND

Ralph shares a pearl of wisdom.

Ralph: I've always followed that old adage, "Be kind to the people you meet on the way up, because you're gonna meet the same people on the way down."
Norton: Boy, how true, how true those words are. "Be kind to the people you meet on the way up, because you're gonna meet the same people on the way down." Happens to me every day in the sewer.

Ralph is razzing a new neighbor, a handsome mambo dancer.

Ralph: Notice the difference between my hands and your hands. That'll show you difference in work. The difference between your hands and my friend's hands.
Norton: Wait a minute, it's not fair to compare his to mine. I got mine in water all day.

Ralph explains the principle of water pressure.

Ralph: It's a simple scientific principle. I hope that you realize that water always seeks its level.
Norton: Yes, we've heard rumors to that effect down the sewer.

Norton meets the press.

Reporter: Your name?
Norton: Edward L. Norton.
Reporter: Your occupation?
Norton: I'm an engineer... in subterranean sanitation.

Norton displays his typing skills for Ralph.

Ralph: Why didn't you get a job in an office instead of taking a job down the sewer?
Norton: Well, I just couldn't stand the thought of being cooped up in a stuffy office.

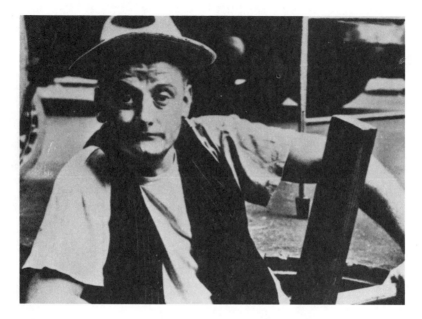

Trixie consoles Norton after he loses his job.

Trixie: Maybe you could try some other kind of work.
Norton: Let's face it, there's not many jobs that I could step into. A sewer worker is like a brain surgeon...we're both specialists!

Ralph's feeling the effects of a strained back.

Ralph: Do you know what it's like to have a hot head and cold feet?
Norton: I know how it is. I get that way any August day in the sewer when it's high tide.

Norton doubts Ralph.

Norton: You got a telephone call from the Grand High Exalted Mystic Ruler, the emperor of all Racoondom? I don't believe it.
Ralph: Sure you don't believe it, because you never got a call from the Grand High Exalted Mystic Ruler.
Norton: He don't have to call me, he works right next to me in the sewer.

Norton's being interviewed.

Reporter: Mr. Norton, tell me something, what kind of work do you do?
Norton: Well, I'm employed by the city.
Reporter: I see, in a white-collar job?
Norton: No, I'd say it was more of a wet-collar job.

Ralph has to learn how to play golf.

Ralph: *You,* tellin' *me* how to play golf?!? Whadda you know about it?
Norton: I know all I need to know about playin' golf. It's a game they play with eighteen holes. I been workin' in the sewers for ten years. If that don't qualify me as an expert on holes, I give up.

Norton thinks he was beaten out of a promotion by someone with connections.

Ralph: He's only been with the company for a year. How could he get close to the big shots?
Norton: Well, don't forget, for the last six months he's been workin' in the sewer right underneath City Hall.

Two teens in the neighborhood are going steady.

Alice: When a girl wears a fella's pin it means she's going steady. She's his and nobody else's.
Norton: I get it. It's like a custom we got, you carve your best girl's initials on the shovel down in the sewer.

Norton "confesses" to the IRS.

Norton: There are a few little items I didn't put down on my income tax form. During the past fiscal year I found three dollars that was floatin' by me in the sewer.

Alice wants to spend a romantic night out with Ralph.

Ralph: She wants to go through the Tunnel of Love. She says that's romantic.

Norton: I've been through the Tunnel of Love, it's not romantic. Wading through that water'n all.

Ralph: How did Trixie like it?

Norton: Trixie wasn't with me. I was down there workin', fixin' a leak in one of the pipes.

Ralph: That isn't exactly what Alice meant. She wants to go through the Tunnel of Love with me.

Norton: Whadda you and Alice know about fixin' leaks?

Norton's lost his job.

Alice: Ed, he fired you?
Norton: How do you like that? Reliable ol' Ed Norton workin' seventeen years in the sewer and now everything down the drain!

Norton describes an occupational hazard.

Norton: I haven't been smokin' cigars so much lately. Too much trouble tryin' to light the wet end.
Brother Racoon: The wet end? You're supposed to light the dry end.
Norton: My boy, in the sewer there ain't no dry end.

Norton plans his son's future.

Norton: Grammar school, high school, and then on to college. And when he gets outta college and is ready to face the world I'll get 'im a job with me in the sewer.
Ralph: When your son graduates from college you're gonna get him a job in the sewer?
Norton: Certainly! The sewer accepts college grads!

Norton has the sniffles.

Norton: Must be catchin' a cold. Probably caught it workin' in that sewer on Park Avenue. Always catch a cold workin' in the Park Avenue sewer.
Ralph: What's so different about a Park Avenue sewer?
Norton: They're air conditioned.

Ralph and Norton attend the reading of a will.

Lawyer: We were about to start without you. There are some things that just can't wait.
Norton: Like we say in the sewer, "Time and tide wait for no man."

Norton introduces a new card game.

Norton: The most important thing you gotta remember about Knuckle Knuckle is that all the wet cards are wild.
Ralph: All the wet cards are wild? What wet cards?
Norton: Well, we usually play this during the lunch hour down the sewer...
Ralph: !#@*!&@*!!#*!

I was telling the guy in the ambulance, "There's nothing wrong with me. I'm not hurt." The only thing that happened to me is the manhole cover landed on my head. That's happened hundreds of times. In the sewer that's an occupational hazard.

Norton and Ralph admire a mounted game fish that Ralph's boss landed in Florida.

Norton: My boss has got one of those in his living room.
Ralph: When was he in Florida?
Norton: Never. He killed it in self-defense down the sewer.

The boys in the sewer are partying.

Ralph: Every time I come to see you in the sewer you're runnin' a celebration of some kind. If I ever did that on my job I'd be fired in a minute. How d'ya get away with it?

Norton: They don't dare fire us. Who they gonna get to replace us?

The Nortons have had their apartment painted and come calling on the Kramdens at 2:00 A.M.

Alice: Trixie said they couldn't sleep because of the smell of the paint. She asked if they could spend the rest of the night with us and I said yes.
Ralph: Boy, that's a hot one! Norton works in the sewer all day and he can't stand the smell of paint!

Ralph thinks he's been offered an important job by someone who got on his bus.

Ralph: Do you think there's anything to what that guy said to me today? Do you think a guy could get a real break that way?
Norton: Yeah, I think there's somethin' in it. A similar thing happened to me once. I was in a diner one day havin' lunch, there's a guy sittin' on a stool next to me, we strike up a conversation. Pretty soon we got to talkin' about the work I was doin'. Then I realize he's interested in me, and right then and there he promises me a better job than the one I had.
Ralph: Did he keep his promise?
Norton: He sure did, that's how I got my job in the sewer.

If pizzas were manhole covers, the sewer would be a paradise!

Norton meets Ralph's boss.

Ralph's boss: Mr. Norton, in what line of business are you?
Norton: I work for the city.
Ralph's boss: In what capacity?
Norton: Capacity? About fifty thousand gallons a day!

The Racoon president can't believe his ears.

Racoon president: You play Ping-Pong in the sewer?!?
Norton: Yeah! It's the only game we can play with a
ball that can float.

Ralph's been laid off.

Norton: I know just how you feel 'cause I went through the same thing when they laid me off in the sewer. I felt just like a fish outta water.

Norton suffers a professional setback.

Alice: You didn't pass the test for sewer inspector.
Norton: No...I washed out.

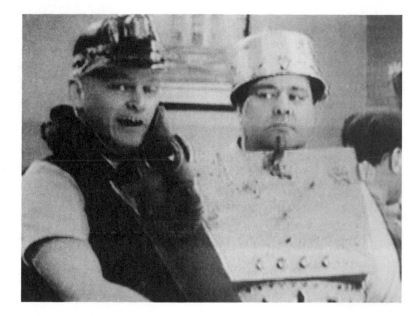

I'm a senior supervisor in subterranean sanitation.

Ralph's out of work.

Norton: Maybe I can get a job for you with me in the sewer. All you have to do is pass the test.
Ralph: What test?
Norton: Can you float?

Ralph and Norton meet for lunch.

Ralph: I had to come all the way down from a hundred and twenty-ninth street and I was here on time. You're in the sewer two blocks away and you can't make it. Why not?
Norton: I couldn't help it, Ralph, the tide was against me all the way.

Ralph and Norton are going to the race track.

Ralph: I'll have to get in touch with the bus depot and tell 'em I'm not comin' in. You better do the same thing.
Norton: I don't have to call the office. All I gotta do is write a note, put it in a milk bottle, and drop it down an open manhole.

Norton meets big band leaders Tommy and Jimmy Dorsey.

Norton: I was wonderin' if maybe you could play for us at the Sewer Workers Fiesta.
Jimmy Dorsey: If we're free. When is it?
Norton: It won't be until summertime. We gotta hold it out in the open. Nobody'll rent us a hall.

*I work hard for the money I earn down in that
sewer. It's no easy job, you know. Some days I get
it right up to here!*

Norton displays some ingenuity.

Norton: That muffler you knitted for me for Christmas came in mighty handy today down the sewer.
Trixie: Oh, was it cold there today?
Norton: No, there was a leak in the main pipe. I used it to plug it up.

Ralph and Norton plan to switch their jobs to the night shift.

Ralph: It won't be so bad, me drivin' a bus at night. At least there'll be less traffic.
Norton: With my job it don't make no difference anyway. Once they put the manhole cover on the sewer you can't tell night from day anyway.

Norton wants a new bill of fare.

Norton: Trixie, will ya stop givin' me Limburger cheese sandwiches for lunch.
Trixie: I thought you liked 'em.
Norton: I do, but the guys down the sewer can't stand the smell.

Norton reflects on having followed his grandfather and father into the sewers.

Norton: You might say there was a Norton underground ever since there were sewers.

Ralph is entering a contest.

Norton: I entered one of these contests once. Another guy and myself had exactly the same answers and he won and I lost.
Ralph: If you had the same answers, why did you lose?
Norton: Well, neatness counted, and I filled out my blank down in the sewer.

Norton ignores the clock.

Alice: Ed, don't you have to go to work?
Norton: No, Alice, I got plenty of time. They're not too particular about punctuality in the sewer. As a matter of fact, they figure it's lucky if we just show up at all.

Norton meets Ralph's boss.

Ralph's boss: How did you ever get a job in the sewer?
Norton: Just lucky, I guess.

The Nortons have been invited out.

Norton: Trixie, guess what? We got an invite from ol' Bruce Hupfelt for cocktails and dinner at his house Wednesday night.
Trixie: Oh, is Bruce back working with you?
Norton: No, he's still workin' in that sewer in East Bronx.
Trixie: Did he call you on the phone?
Norton: No, he put a note in a bottle, it come floatin' by today.

Norton and Ralph discuss their tax returns.

Norton: You mean you can take off to have your work clothes cleaned and pressed?
Ralph: Of course you can.
Norton: What a deduction I got, boy. I got not only cleanin' and pressin', I got fumagatin' too!

Ralph has broken his leg in a bus accident.

Norton: With a thing like that you're lucky, you can collect. I had an accident once, couldn't collect a thin dime. They claimed I didn't even have a case.

Ralph: What kind of an accident?

Norton: I was workin' in the sewer and a manhole cover fell on my head.

Ralph: Well, why couldn't you collect?

Norton: I couldn't prove it did any damage.

Norton tries to console Ralph.

Ralph: I lost my job.
Norton: Sorry to hear about that, Ralph. Wish I could get you a job workin' with me down the sewer, but they're not takin' on any unskilled laborers.

Norton needs an idea for a gift.

Norton: One of the boys I work with is retirin' after thirty years in the sewer and I've been elected as head of the committee to buy him a gift. I'm tryin' to get some ideas.
Alice: Gee, I don't know, Ed. What would be a good gift?
Norton: I submitted a suggestion that wasn't too warmly received.
Alice: Oh, what was that?
Norton: Well, I thought it would be a nice touch if we had his rubber boots bronzed.

Ralph is keeping Norton up all night writing songs.

Norton: I gotta get up early, I got a job to do.
Ralph: Well, I got a job to do, you don't hear me beefin' about havin' to go to bed. And I got responsibilities. If I fall asleep I'm liable to run into somethin'.
Norton: If I fall asleep I'm liable to drown!

Norton on the prospect of being a father.

Norton: I always wanted a son to follow after me, someone to wade in my footsteps.

Ralph and Norton are cleaning up.

Ralph: Let's start with these dishes. Do you wanna wash or dry?
Norton: I'll wash. I might as well, I got my hands in water all day anyway.

Norton has bought perfume for Trixie.

Norton: I hope it smells good.
Ralph: Whaddya mean, don't you know how it smells?
Norton: No, I haven't any sense of smell. You think I'd work in the sewer if I did?

Ralph has a secret.

Ralph: Don't you tell Trixie anything about this. She'll blab it to Alice and ruin the whole thing.
Norton: Whaddya mean, you're talkin' to a guy who can keep a secret. I'm an expert at that. Down the sewer we got a slogan about it…"Keep your mouth shut!"

After a fight with Trixie, Norton wants to sleep at Ralph's but Ralph won't let him.

Ralph: Out, out, ouuut!
Norton: Have a heart. I can't go back upstairs, I can't go out in the street like this, where am I gonna go?
Ralph: Open up a manhole, sleep in the sewer.
Norton: I can't do that! Ordinance 4082 section 5 paragraph b, "The city sewers can't be used for personal pleasure!"

One of Norton's co-workers needs some money, fast.

Ralph: Wait a minute! What could a guy possibly want down in the sewer that he needs two bucks right away?

Norton: It's like this, you see, today's payday and during lunch hour the guys got a little dice game goin' on down there...you might call it a floatin' crap game.

What did I know about my job before I joined the Department of Sanitation? I didn't know a sewer from a hole in the ground.

TRIXIE, MARRIAGE, AND THE OPPOSITE SEX

Ralph: What does a woman fall for better than anything else?
Norton: A left hook.

The Racoons are throwing a bachelor party for Stanley Saxon.

Stanley Saxon: I know that all of you must have been joking about the things you said about marriage tonight. I'm very happy.
Norton: That's cause you ain't married yet. Wait'll tomorrow!

Norton is jealous of a handsome new neighbor.

Norton: You better get to know Trixie and me pretty fast because we may be movin' tomorrow.
Neighbor: Oh really? Trixie never mentioned it.
Norton: Trixie don't know it yet.

Ralph wants Norton to get Trixie out of his apartment.

Norton: Trix, don't you think you better go upstairs?
Trixie: What for?
Norton: To put a beefsteak on that black eye.
Trixie: What black eye?
Norton: The one you're gonna get if you don't go upstairs and put a beefsteak on it!

Norton recalls when he courted Trixie.

Norton: I remember when I first met Trixie. She was dancin' in a burlesque show. I used to wait for her backstage every night. When she'd come to work I'd give her a rose.
Ralph: Did she wear it?
Norton: She had to, it was her costume.

Norton won't help Trixie hem a dress.

Trixie: All right, Ed, but someday you're gonna ask me to do something for you.
Norton: I'm asking you right now...leave the premises!

Norton realizes that a scheme to sell a kitchen gadget on TV has been a colossal flop.

Norton: If my wife Trixie's lookin' in and when I get home she says "I told you so" I'm gonna belt her right in the mouth!

*This is my lucky jacket. One day I was goin'
down the street wearin' this jacket, I found five
bucks. That was lucky. One day I went to the
horse races, bet on every race, won every race.
That was lucky. I was also wearin' this jacket the
night I met Trixie. Well, two outta three ain't
bad!*

Norton gives Ralph advice.

Norton: Why don't you just put your foot down and say "Alice, I'm goin' bowlin'."
Ralph: Getta load of who's talking. How about the night Trixie insisted that you go with her to her mother's house the night we were gonna play pool.
Norton: Well, we ended up playing pool, didn't we?
Ralph: Yeah. You and me against her and her mother.

Ralph is advising his friend against moving in with his wife's parents after his wedding.

Groom-to-be: Agnes was very definite about it. I don't want to argue.
Norton: Well, if you don't want to argue, what're you gettin' married for?

Norton's been fired.

Norton: You and Trix've been friends for a long time. Suppose you go upstairs and break the news to her.
Alice: Oh no Ed, that's a man's job.
Norton: You're right Alice...I'll get Ralph to do it.

Norton plays Sir Galahad.

Alice: I've gotta go up and get some laundry off the roof.

Norton: Wait a minute. Is there a lot of laundry up there?

Alice: Quite a bit.

Norton: Well, you don't think I'm gonna stand here and watch you carry a big load of laundry down here all by yourself, do ya?

Alice: Oh, thanks Ed.

Norton: Don't thank me. Trixie, go up there and give her a hand!

Ralph needs a loan.

Ralph: Will you lend me fifteen bucks?

Norton: Gee, Ralph, I'd like to help you out but yesterday I bought a present for Trixie and spent my last cent. You know how it is with women, once in a while you gotta buy 'em a present to prove you still love 'em.

Ralph: What'd you get her?

Norton: A new broom.

Norton knocks Trixie's cooking.

Norton: I wish Trixie could make icing that tastes like this.
Alice: Icing?!? Ed, that's starch!
Norton: Starch? I still wish Trixie could make icing that tastes like this.

Norton has indigestion.

Trixie: Supper all right, Ed?
Norton: Well, let me give you a little hint, Trixie. I wouldn't advise you to take part in the Pillsbury Bake-off next year.

Ralph is late and Alice is worried.

Norton: I read in the papers every day where guys run away.
Trixie: What reason does Ralph have to run away?
Norton: He's married, ain't he?

Ralph has run into an old friend.

Ralph: Did you get married?
Friend: Nah.
Norton: No? How come you look so sad?

The Nortons are fighting.

Trixie: Let me tell you something, Edward Norton, before I even met you there were five men after me to get married.
Norton: Yeah, your father, your three brothers, and your Uncle Julius who supported all of ya!

Norton and Trixie have different ideas about their vacation.

Alice: Trixie has her heart set on going to Atlantic City.
Norton: Don't worry about a thing. She'll go where I go.
Alice: Yeah? What're you gonna tell her if she puts up a squawk?
Norton: Very simple, I know what to say. I'll just tell 'er Atlantic City is *closed* for the summer.

Norton advises a newlywed-to-be.

Norton: May your life be rosy and bright. If you take the advice of an old married man you will get outta town tonight!

Alice has returned from visiting her mother.

Ralph: How's your mother, sweetie?
Alice: Much better, just a cold.
Ralph: I want you to know that it was pretty lonely around here without you.
Trixie: Oh Ed, why don't you ever talk to me like that?
Norton: I'd be very happy to if you'd only go away once in a while!

Norton gets "plastered."

Norton: Hey Alice, what is this, coconut cream or meringue?
Alice: It isn't that at all, it's plaster for a hole in the bedroom ceiling.
Norton: I just ate some.
Alice: Do you feel sick?
Norton: Nah, I don't feel sick, I'm used to it. I been eatin' this stuff for years, only Trixie calls it biscuits.

The Kramdens and Nortons are arguing.

Trixie: Every mistake Ed's made Ralph has talked him into.

Ralph: Is that so? Well I didn't talk him into marryin' you, did I?

Trixie: Ed, did you hear what he said?

Norton: He's got us there, he didn't.

The wives want Norton and Ralph to spend more time with them.

Ralph: We're entitled to our own enjoyment. Even the Constitution says that a man is entitled to life, liberty, and the pursuit of happiness!
Norton: Yeah, but the marriage license is an amendment to the Constitution.

Ralph has arranged a date for Alice's aunt with the local butcher.

Ralph: Freddie, let me ask you something. Why didn't you ever get married?
Freddie: I don't know myself, Ralph. But I wanna tell you one thing, this single life is murder. I gotta spend every night alone or I gotta go out by myself. One night it's bowling, one night it's the ballgame, another night I go over to Jersey and see a burlesque show, and Friday night's the fights.
Ralph: Well, why didn't ya ever get married?
Norton: Never mind that. How come we didn't stay single?

Ralph needs Norton's money for another scheme.

Ralph: You're goin' tomorrow and gettin' that money.
Norton: Look, Ralph, it ain't as easy as all that. Our money is in a joint account.
Ralph: So what if it's in a joint account. That money is just as much yours as it is hers.
Norton: Well, there's a little technicality involved there. Our joint account is in the name of Trixie and her mother.

The Nortons are fighting and Ralph's trying to help.

Trixie: Get him outta here, I'm sorry I ever met him!

Norton: You're sorry you ever met me, huh? For your information, I could've married Cora Brenstetter, and her father is a pretty big man downtown. He told me that the day I married her he'd have me transferred from the Department of Sewers. I never threw this in your face before, but if I hadda married Cora Brenstetter, *today* I woulda been drivin' my own garbage truck!

A prowler's on the loose and Norton has left Trixie alone.

Alice: All I know is, if I was upstairs with Trixie I'd be mighty scared.
Norton: Don't worry about Trixie, she's armed. She's standin' by the door with a frying pan.
Ralph: A fryin' pan? That's no weapon.
Norton: It is when she cooks.

Norton: A house is like a woman. A little paint here, a little paint there, you never know how broken down she really is.

I don't get that wife of mine. All the time puttin'
cologne, powder, perfume on. I mean after all,
I'm the one that works in the sewer!

NORTON'S WORDS TO LIVE BY

As you slide down the
bannister of life, may the
splinters never be pointin' the
wrong way.

When the tides of life turn against you, and the current upsets your boat, don't waste those tears on what might have been, just lay on your back and float.

Ralph, I guess you and me is just a couple of hangnails on the Fickle Finger of Fate.

One of my most important principles, to wit: Never to interfere or meddle or become embroiled with another family's mish mosh.

What do I need a wife for? A man's best companion, a man's best friend is his bowling ball. Always with ya, never gets ya into trouble, no backtalk, always goes wherever you wanna take it, never kicks when you leave it at home, never nags at ya when the bowling ball next door gets a fur jacket. Through the highways and byways of life all a man needs is his bowling ball.

I, Edward Norton, Ranger Third Class in the Captain
Video Space Academy, do solemnly pledge to obey my
mommy and daddy, be kind to dumb animals and old
ladies in and out of space, not to tease my little
brothers and sisters, and to brush my teeth twice a day
and drink milk after every meal.